It's Easy To Play
Richard Clayderman.

Wise Publications
London/New York/Sydney

4·95

Exclusive Distributors:
Music Sales Limited
8/9 Frith Street, London W1V 5TZ, England.
Music Sales Pty. Limited
120 Rothschild Avenue, Rosebery, NSW 2018, Australia.

This book © Copyright 1986 by
Wise Publications
ISBN 0.7119.0795.1
Order No. AM 61599

Art direction by Mike Bell
Cover illustration by Jenny Powell
Arranged by Frank Booth
Compiled by Frank Booth

Music Sales complete catalogue lists thousands
of titles and is free from your local music
book shop, or direct from Music Sales Limited.
Please send a cheque or Postal Order for £1.50 for postage to
Music Sales Limited, 8/9 Frith Street, London W1V 5TZ, England.

Printed in England by
Eyre & Spottiswoode Limited, London and Margate

Dolannes Melodie

Composer: Paul de Senneville

Bright waltz tempo

Fmaj7

C7

F

Fmaj7

C7

F

Fmaj7

C7

F

Fmaj7

6

7

Only You

Words and Music by Vincent Clarke

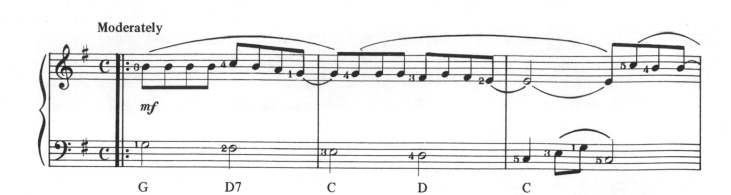

Strangers In The Night

Music by Bert Kaempfert
Words by Charles Singleton and Eddie Snyder

rit.

G7

a tempo

E♭

G♭dim

Fm   Fm(7♯)   Fm7   Fm6   Fm

Bb7

Eb

Ebmaj7   Eb

f

Bbm

C7(b9)

Fm

Abm

Eb   Cm7   Fm   Bb7

Eb

rall.

Bb7

Eb

13

Jardin Secret

Composer: Paul de Senneville

Romantica Serenade

Composer: Paul de Senneville and Olivier Toussaint

G7

C

E

Am

D(sus4)

D7

G

B7

Em

G

18

G7(sus4)　　　G7　　　　C

E

Am

D(sus4)

Repeat ad lib. and Fade

D

19

My Way

Words by Paul Anka
Music by Claude Francois and Jacques Revaux

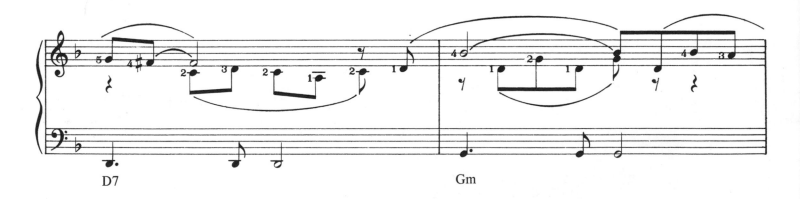

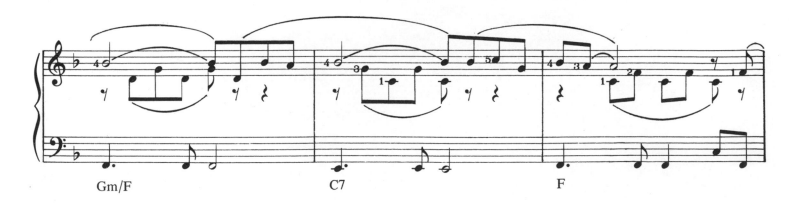

Fmaj7

Cm7/F

F7(♭9)

B♭

Gm7(♭5)

F

Gm7/C

C7

Gm7/F

1.

2.

3

F

F

C9

F

Fmaj7

cresc. poco a poco

Cm7/F

F7(♭9)

B♭

21

B♭maj7   B♭6 F Gm7

C7   Am   Dm

To Coda ⊕

Gm7   C7

D.%. al Coda

Gm7   F

⊕ *CODA*

rit.   *ff*   *p*

C7   Gm7/F   F
                  Ped. _____ *

Voyage A Venise

Composer: Olivier Toussaint

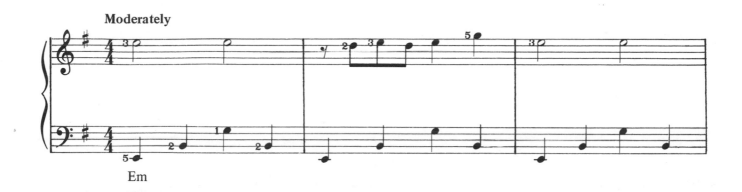

Am   Em   Am

To Coda ⊕

Em   Am   Em

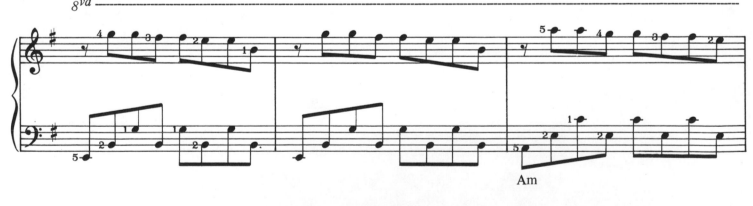

Am

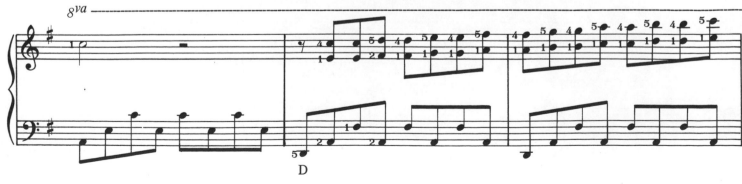

D

25

L'Enfant Et La Mer

Composer: Paul de Senneville and Olivier Toussaint

Moderately

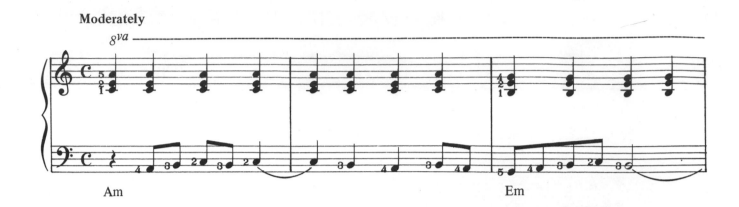

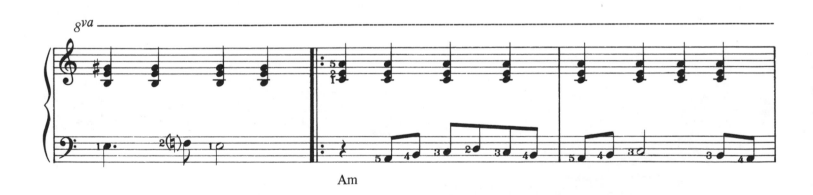

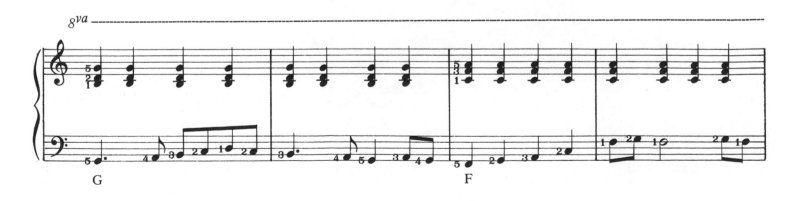

Love Is Blue (L'Amour Est Bleu)

Music by Andre Popp
Original Words by Pierre Cour
English Lyric by Bryan Blackburn

D D7 G   Em   C   B7   Em

mp

E   B9   E

Ped ————————————————————— * Ped. ——————————————— *

A   E   G#m

(Ped. sim.)

A6   B7(sus4)   B7   E

f

Em   A   D   D7   G

29

30

Greensleeves

Arranger: Olivier Toussaint and Gerard Salesses

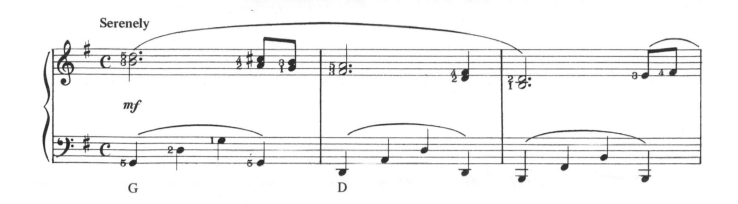

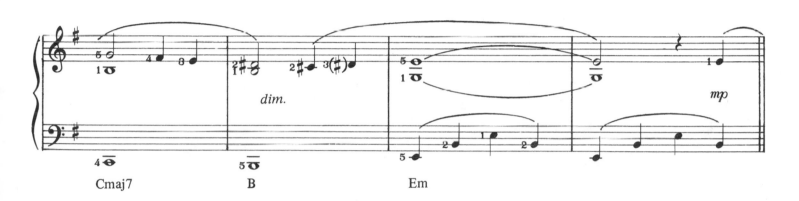

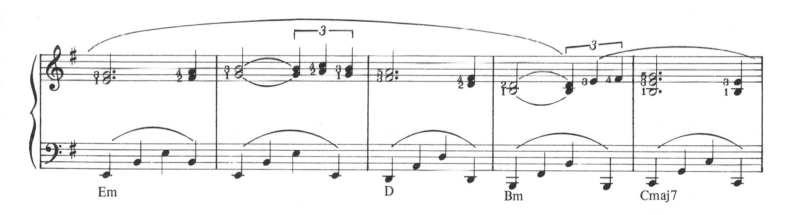

Em

D

Bm

Cmaj7

B7

Em

G

D

C

B7

Bsus4

B7

G

32

As Time Goes By

Words and Music by Herman Hupfeld

F   B♭   B♭m   F   F7   B♭

D7   Gm   A♭dim

Dim   B♭7   Gm7(♭5)   G7   Gm7   F♯dim

D.%. al Coda

⊕ *CODA*

C7   C7   F♯dim

Gm7   C7+   Fmaj9

Ped. ————————————————————————————————— *

Ballade Pour Adeline

Composer: Paul de Senneville

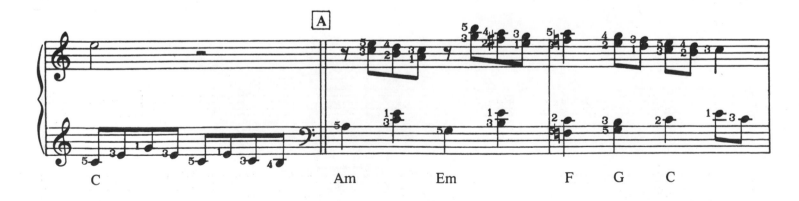

Am   Em   F   G   G7

C   Dm

G   C E♭   F   G7   C

To A

Dm   G   C

2   To B   3   8
C   F G   C   F G   C   F G   C
                                        rall.
                                        Ped   *

37

La Vraie Musique De L'Amour

Composer: Paul de Senneville

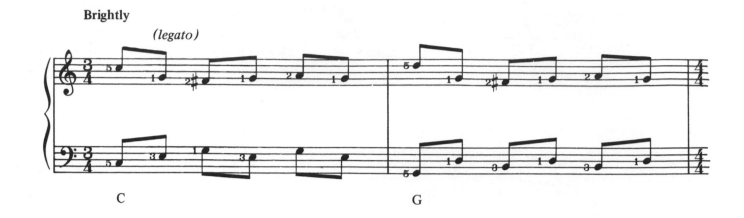

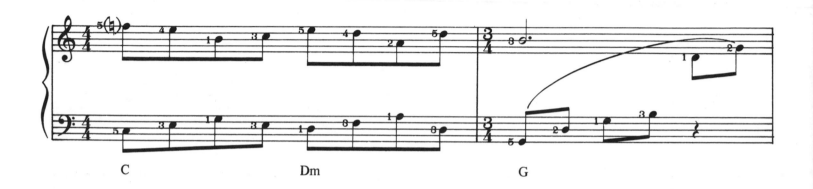

39

41

Yesterday

Words and Music by John Lennon and Paul McCartney

Fsus4   F   C   Dm   G   B♭   F

Em7/A   A7   Dm C B♭ Dm Gm C

F   Em7sus4   A7   Dm C B♭ Dm

8va ——————— *loco*

Gm   C   F   F

Ped. — — — — — — — — — — *

Em7   A7   Dm   C B♭ C

43

Fsus4   F C Dm   G

Bb   F   F

Em7   A7   Dm   C Bb   C

Fsus4   F C Dm   G   Bb   F

8va —

Dm F   G   Bb   F

L'Amour Exile

Composer: Olivier Toussaint

C7   F

C7   F   F

Bb   G7   C   Bb   A

D   Ab7   Db   G7   C7

A little faster

F7   Bbm

47

Checklist of important piano books.

The books below are available from your local music shop who will order them for you if not in stock.
If there is no music shop near you, you may order direct from Music Sales Limited (Dept. M), 8/9 Frith Street, London, W1V 5TZ.
Please always include £1·00 to cover post/packing costs.

A Start At The Piano
AM 40650

Alison Bell's Graded For Piano Pieces Book 1: Very Easy
AM 30297

Book 5: Upper Intermediate
AM 30339

Anthology Of Piano Music Volume 1: Baroque
AM 10968

Volume 3: Romantic
AM 10984

Barrelhouse And Boogie Piano
OK 64659

Big Note Piano Book 1
AM 28226

Bud Powell: Jazz Masters Series
AM 23219

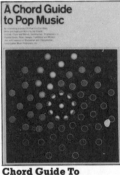

Chord Guide To Pop Music
AM 10596

The Classic Piano Repertoire Bach
EW 50023

Chopin
EW 50015

Promenade Theory Papers Book 1
PB 40583

Classics To·Moderns Book 1
YK 20014

Classics To Moderns Sonatas & Sonatinas
YK 20204

Themes & Variations
YK 20196

More Classics To Moderns Book 1
YK 20121

Dave Brubeck: Jazz Masters Series
AM 21189

Easy Classical Piano Duets
AM 31949

The Complete Piano Player By Kenneth Baker Book 1
AM 34828

Book 2
AM 34836

Book 3
AM 34844

Book 4
AM 34851

Book 5
AM 34869

Style Book
AM 35338